LET'S NOT
LIVE
ON EARTH

Sarah Blake

LET'S NOT
LIVE
ON EARTH

Wesleyan University Press   Middletown, Connecticut

Wesleyan Poetry

Wesleyan University Press
Middletown CT 06459
www.wesleyan.edu/wespress
© 2018 Sarah Blake
All rights reserved
Manufactured in the United States of America
Designed by Mindy Basinger Hill
Typeset in Parkinson Electra Pro

Library of Congress Cataloging-in-Publication Data available upon request

Hardcover ISBN: 978-0-8195-7766-5
Paperback ISBN: 978-0-8195-7765-8
Ebook ISBN: 978-0-8195-7767-2

5   4   3   2   1

If you were lost, I would cry, my son says to me.

If you were lost, I would cry, I say back to him.

CONTENTS

Q

LET'S NOT
LIVE
ON EARTH

SUICIDE PREVENTION

New signs at all the local train stations—
Suicide Prevention Lifeline.

I'm glad my son can't read yet.

Yesterday morning he made up a friend, Lofty,
who was captured by bad guys.

My husband asked, *Loffy?*

He said, *No, with a T.*
If it was a v, it would be Lof-vee.
He's starting to get it.

If it was a circle, it would be Lof-circle.
He's almost starting to get it.

Today he tells me he's dead. He's a ghost.
He misses his ghost family.
Something's wrong because they're inside
the wall but he can't get through.

Then he walks into the wall to show me.

Then a ghost ladybug shows up who can get
through the wall, and he saves everyone.

My son bends down to hug a family
of very small ghosts.

I don't know how to talk to him about death.

When I told him about his great grandfather,
who he's named after, and that conversation
led right where you think—*He's dead*—

he told me, *Only bad guys die*, and I
could only argue that so many times.

Before I tell my son about suicide, I want to
tell him about murder, I want to tell him
about dying of an illness, about dying in sleep.

It feels awful to hold that plan inside me,
to know this ranking of death.

Do I tell him about genocide last? Or
how you keep hearing for a few minutes
after you die? How I'd like him to play me
a nice song and repeat that he loves me.

How he better tell me first
if he wants to take his life because
I would understand that.

I've understood that for a long time.

RETRIBUTION

What if you owed sadness and so
became it?

Are you not indebted to everyone?

I'm asking
what if the debt were sadness?

What if when we walked,
we didn't say,

this is Gaia's breast,
but, *this is her sadness*,

and the mountains made sense,
all the moving plates,

earthquakes and volcanoes?
She pays it forward

and you'll pay it back.
You will lose your body to

sadness at a point
like a temperature

and then you will wake and wake
and wake and wake and wake to it.

THE E-RAY IS A GUN

My son is asking where his gun is and talking about needing to build his bomb, but it's not what you think.

This episode of Batman has a gorilla villain who uses a gun and a bomb to turn humans into super-evolved gorillas like him.

So now my son carries around a plastic Fisher-Price golf bag and calls it his e-ray, for evolution ray, and points it at us, *KSHH*.

My husband, Batman, gets his hand on the e-ray, changes the setting, and uses it to turn my son into a human. And he cries.

He's acting, but it's good, in that it's sad. So my husband changes him back and my son dances around the kitchen.

Later I'm crying in bed watching Cake Boss because Buddy recreated the top tier of his wedding cake for his wife on their anniversary and handmade all the sugar flowers, and she cared about that.

Not that I'm judging her. I'd like to be a woman delighted by cake. I'd like to be a woman who's eaten a sugar flower.

Gum paste flower. Modeling chocolate flower. Buttercream flower. My mouth full of them. My husband's mouth full of them. My son's mouth full of them.

No—I'm hoping there's a woman that's at ease somewhere. So at ease in her life.

ONE DOCTOR LEADS
TO THE NEXT

Today a nurse told me
my uterus felt large.
Can you imagine
sticking your fingers
in and determining
of that slickness
anything? It's so fast
usually—the fingers in,
the pushes on the belly,
uterus, ovary, ovary,
done. Pronounced fine
or great or all good
here, one machine of my
many-machined body.
Sometimes a finger in
my anus too, another
angle, and I don't know,
I'm a small woman
with a big ass arranged
on a table, so ok, just
ok. Find everything
small and positioned.
Find everything in what
I could not. Fingers up
there plenty and it feels
like when I dissected
a squid in middle school,

only, if it hadn't been dead,
if it were strong. She
paused today. At the top
of my uterus she pressed
again and again.
Now I have to call for
an ultrasound for fibroids
that may have made
my uterus large. Broken
bell ringing in the body
I could've sworn
was made of gears.

MOTHERS

Once I heard a mother on the subway say to her toddler, *If you walk away one more time, I'm going to punch you in the leg.* The kid kept smiling.

Today my son is sitting on my lap at school in the morning, and a boy gets close to us, points to my son's belly and names him over and over.

My son slaps him softly across his face.

No hitting! That's not ok! He was being nice. We don't hit. Are you ok? The boy looks the same as ever. Dopey, gentle, fine.

I know people are judging me as a mother all the time.

I THOUGHT IT WAS A GOOD IDEA
TO WALK TO CVS WITH MY SON
ON A NINETY-DEGREE DAY

First we go to the Rita's next door. The plastic spoon slices that flesh
    inside my lips—
because you wouldn't call that skin, right? The rest of the day I run my
    tongue over the slices,
which remind me of the shape of the spoon, as if it's in my mouth again.

We waited so long at CVS, I bought my son a coloring book that was on
    sale.
You color in a page, then you use an app on your phone to transform it.
    They call it 4D
as if everyone's an idiot.

For the walk home, we take nine smaller roads. I catch sight of a ground-
    down stump
to the right of the sidewalk. Only then do I see branches piled high to the
    left. Just like that
we're walking through a body like it's nothing.

I complain to my husband on the phone about how I can't get the stroller
over the broken cement of someone's driveway. Only then do I see
    someone sitting in the yard
within earshot. I want to apologize. I want to say, *It's like mine.*

But it's too late. I'm a bitch at the end of a three-mile walk after my
    insurance almost
denied coverage for my anxiety medication.
I think my anxiety isn't mine at all. I think it's communal.

I know they've found that we inherit trauma, but what about when there's
    no time to pass it
between generations. What then?
At home, we drink water. We're covered in sweat. We color in a dragon.

With the app, he flies above the page, the color my son gave his skin,
his head turning as if he heard my son's voice, until he does it over and
    over, predictable
little dragon head. Whole predictable body.

We'll all be sleeping tonight, at some point. At some point,
we'll all be sleeping tonight. Unless we die in these last hours of the day.
But if we make it through, my head will look like yours, asleep. Just like it.
    Just like that.

EVERYTHING SMALL

Look, ok, the story—
first, a fox
is on fire, but not
dying, no, in a god-
like way, and flying
a bit, you know,
in the yard
above the grass
in a figure eight
loosely,
and grinning
so maybe you look
at the fox and think,
He's a fool!
except that you're
distracted by
all the fire,
how you feel heat
from him from
inside the house
where you've been
all along,
haven't you?

But to continue—
second, a rabbit,
small enough
to hide beneath
a weed,

one leaf of a weed,
which is sad,
yes, pity the body
before it's grown
fully, or
the body that
can't complete
itself how it might,
not that
everything small
is paltry, just
worry about
the rabbit for me
who's in the yard
right now
under that fiery fox
that came
out of nowhere.

Shit, you left
the house
with a treat in your
hand as if you
understand foxes,
fox-gods, any
wild animal
in forms magical,
impossible.
Throw it away from
the rabbit, go to
the rabbit—
is that the plan,

the rescue that
paints you
hero, savior?
Well, the fox comes
right up and
bites your hand off.
How's that, you
wonder, you
handless fiend?
The rabbit's gone.

And the fox,
sated or feeling
bad about what
he's done,
is off, down the hill,
flame going out,
feet touching
ground again,
slipping into
the gallop of every
four-legged animal
that comes
to about the knee,
his soft ears
turning
at the sound of
your voice
screaming
but starting to cry.
Every animal
nearby, you imagine,
is turning to listen
to you now.

TWO OAKS

I remember them as impossible trees—roots perfectly under the ground. I have a maple tree now and you can't grow anything at its base, such a wreck with its knotty roots, and I see the way the animals burrow there, in that patch of dirt. But my childhood backyard is a flat field of zoysia in my mind, hardly touched by the two trees, as if they poked through a plane of existence, connecting one plane to another, the plane of sky maybe, or something before that, just there, just so. If I could plan a dream, I would walk myself up one of those oak trees and touch that next plane. I would pierce it as perfectly as the tree had pierced the plane of grass. I would get all my nutrients from below it but excel above. One unfairness to pile on the others.

RATS

It's difficult to tell
rats are in the basement.
They're so quiet.
We go to bed so early.
After midnight, they
crawl out of a tunnel
and go to the neighbor's
birdfeeder and pond.
I imagine their bodies
in the moonlight,
the reflection of their
small faces in the pond
over the ledge
of flagstones.
After the poison
is placed in our rafters,
we tell the neighbors
the rats might feel
sick and go for water
and die in their pond.
I can see that too.
I looked up pictures
of rats so I can
see them in any
compromised position,
like the naked woman
we can all call up
for any crime
in the news. Just as

I can see them,
the rats now, in
positions of success,
quiet and warm in a nest
between my floorboards.
Their faces the same
in victory and death.
Small as the red globe
grapes that leave
my mouth so sweet
this summer.

FOR MAX

Ok, so you know someone who died horrifically

Ok, so you know an animal who died horrifically

In a fire let's say or a building's collapse

Or, ok, so you know someone who's dying right now

Except maybe not horrifically

Except your idea of horrifically is changing

The way a gun death seemed less horrific than the gas chambers

Until the country kept ignoring gun deaths

Now they seem horrific

And then I really try to consider the word *horrific*

And horror and I think about how I only watch horror movies

In black neighborhoods where they make jokes

The whole time about the dumb white girl that's going back into the house

Until I'm pealing with laughter in my seat

And I think so much of my country, they are dumb white girls going back

Into the house, except they're men, too, and I'm offended by

The attribution of feminine qualities or I'm offended

By the qualities deemed feminine because I'm one tough bitch

Who never has to be one because I don't leave the house

I don't know if I'm mourning you before you die

I don't know if language can write me away or into anything

I'm a butterfly. I'm a pig. I was never in a body to begin with.

I remember as a child trying to think of what animal

I wanted to come back as and not being able to think of one

Because everything is prey to something and my luck

As a human seemed too great, irreplicable, next time I'd for sure

Be a child kidnapped or molested or abused

A mother on her way out of the Y last night told another mother

How she pinches her son because she doesn't know what else to do
And then makes a joke about how she's going to kill him
And it's not a fucking joke, it's not one
And I wonder if that would be a horrific death just because
It's his mother committing the act
That seems like enough even if the death itself isn't torturous
Or inhumane, and I don't know what to do with that word anymore
Because almost every action I've seen lately lacks compassion
And every life I've seen lately has misery in it
Last night a man in my area tried to run a woman's child over
Then got out of his car and said, "You dirty Jew, I should kill all of you.
I should come back with a gun and kill all of you."
There are a lot of reasons for people to point a gun at me I guess
I might die before you I guess
Because that's our country right now and either way
We'll die without each other a little
And if I come back as a cricket, I'll seek out the bird
If I come back as a mouse, I'll seek out the fox
I could do this cycle a hundred times and still enjoy it

A THREAT

I answered the door to a young man.
He looked relieved. And then lustful.

He stepped aside as if to make
a place for me to stand beside him.

I realized quickly that I was the lady.
And if that were true, then nearby

there was a door quite like mine,
and behind it, frantic, livid, the tiger.

MOUTHS AT THE PARTY

For a second, the light
made that glass in her mouth
look like a knife.

I'm embarrassed I thought it.

The woman's injury
in my mind before she'd even
undone her lips.

But my shame is not my
violent tendency,
though I hide them the same,

near my heart. Which is to say,
in my breasts, large
like hers. Who would notice

the blood in our mouths?

THE SAFETY OF WOMEN

Women are not often killed in the street.
They are most often killed in the home.

At every doctor's appointment, I'm asked,
Do you feel safe at home? The woman

who should answer, *No*, most likely ends up
dead—shot, if we're going to be specific.

And I want to be specific, when every vague
word seems to hurt me, when it's thought

the surface speaks to everything needed
to be said because the woman works

on her surface alone. Look at my dancing
on my own skin. Even the shell of me

resembles nothing you could touch me to
with words. Reach out elsewhere, your hand.

YOU ARE CONNECTED TO EVERYTHING

When I Googled, "graveyard hill burning japan earthquake,"
I found a man's stomach, a man's excessive scar, three-
armed, touching in the center like a child's first drawing

of a star, captioned by his brother as, "the scars of 3
liver transplants over a period of 17 years," and it's not
the first time a wound reminded me of the night sky, or

made me think of the word *terrible* as when describing
the plague that killed livestock, and I did think of this man
as an animal, in asking if the skin heals, as my own scar,

that gave way to another body, sits neatly purple, nearly
beneath me (if it were not so central), and the body such
a fine creation to be called the body, because it's been

written, too, the body of a death or the body of heaven—
this seems to be both—this man, not quite, not yet, broken.

MONSTERS

1

This is another story of a monster.
You know how it goes.
There's a young lady. She dies.
There's a child. He dies.
There's a black man. He dies.
The quiet town is disturbed.

2

Boom boom boom. Monster feet.
Chomp chomp chomp. Monster teeth.

Get undressed for bed.
He's watching but it's ok because
a monster's not a man. Not a stranger.

You can name him, can't you?

3

Take the fox
Give him a surprising amount of teeth
He's a monster fox

Take the fish
Give him a surprising amount of teeth
You get the idea

4

"I'm scared," you say.

The monster replies, "Nice to meet you, Scared. I'm a monster."

Because the monster is father to another monster.

The younger monster would have acknowledged your fear.

The younger monster would have been quicker with you.

5

Fee Fi Fo Fum
A giant's not a monster

Even I can be monstrous
And trees (and rivers and planes and flowers and medicine and ants and
  rain and keys and)

A monster is not threats
Not resentful

My nose is swelling with my human smell

6

Sea monsters are easy to draw.
First the water's surface.

Then the snake-like body rising
above it in little mounds
until the edge of the paper

so you can't draw the head,

which isn't glistening anyway
because it's been in the sun
too long, leading the body,

which is good
because then you can't mistake it for a pretty thing.

7

Sometimes monsters are a danger to
Your dead self
Your spirit floating around
Trying to get somewhere
Maybe your child's dream
Because who do you love more
And then,
        monster

8

Today, when I drove to work, I craned my neck.
Then I wondered if I actually checked my blind spot
or just observed how the sun caught in my glasses.

This is how monsters feel when they scare people,
when they rape women, when they eat children.

What was intent? What was the radiant splendor of the day?

9

The princesses thought they were dancing with princes
when they were dancing with monsters,

but that doesn't mean the nights weren't good.

I never understood the danger if
nothing bad ever happened.

I never understood why nothing bad ever happened
if they were monsters.

10

A chimera is terrifying. No extra parts, just disparate.
Giant head of a bat, let's say, and body of a walrus.
Or giant head of a piranha and body of a gorilla.
Or the head of any animal and the body of a man.
Or is it the headless body of a woman that's scarier?
The dissonance between her breasts and her new mouth
of sharper teeth.

11

I know a zombie is a monster—
frightening, imaginary—

but a zombie is too close
to human. Ill-preserved body,

but body all the same. Simple.
Like you. Two arms, two legs.

You look like a zombie.
God damn it.

God damn it.
God damn it.

Here I am loving your face
and you look like one.

12

If monsters were real,
they'd get sick.

They'd have toothaches
and stomachaches
and they'd cough.

Their monster mothers
would watch their fevers,
stay up and sing to them.

If they died,
one long tongue would roll out
of their monster mouth.

Then another.

13

I never understood—

Do vampires suck the blood
through their eye teeth?

Do their teeth become long, sharp,
and hollow?

Do they connect to some unknown
place in the body that must

be newly maintained by blood and thus
eternal life?

Is eternal life just a part of us
that's been abandoned by capillaries?

All we need—
a shock of blood.

14

I forgot about the misplaced body parts.
Extra, disparate, misplaced.

Remember the eyes in the monsters' palms.
How scared you were.

So many new ways to wake a body
if the eyes are in the hands.

Think, too, if you lifted your baby's shirt
and found eyes in the soft skin there.

Think if you found a mouth
chewing quietly on the hem.

15

When the house begins to smell like shit
from the diapers collecting in the trash,
I begin to wonder what the monster's house
smells like: Blood. Bone. Hair. Old meat.
It's the worst smell to imagine. It's worse
to imagine a young monster being raised
accustomed to it, despite a mother always
tying off the trash when the meals are done.

What can you do? Not eat? No. You eat.

16

There's no good animation for a man
turning into a werewolf.

The cut to the hands getting hairy.
The cut back to the man, now hunched.

The attempt at the face
growing a snout.

And we need the snout because we need
the thick wrinkling at the footsteps
of a woman.

Because the desire to eat her
will be as great
as the desire to rape her.

As a monster, you can do both.

17

Monster. Sea monster. Vampire. Werewolf. Zombie. Chimera. Dragon.

Maybe I'm just trying to figure out what you call a man with a gun.
Maybe this is avoidance.

18

Part of me wants to take back
what I said about giants.

The sheer size of their teeth
might be enough.

And their voice, their steps,
even their fat fingers.

But them living in the clouds—
it's so preposterous.

It's hard to fear what can't exist,

that which takes only a simple
understanding of clouds.

The other monsters, I can
picture them.

I see them asleep in their homes,
kicking off their sheets.

19

A monster grows a little monster in you
that makes your chest feel like shit
as it eats your esophagus from the belly up
and it shakes your heart and pulls
on that artery that runs up your neck
until it feels awful to be alive
in your scared and rattled body and
what are you going to do—cry about it?

The monster under my bed
doesn't come out anymore.
I grew up and he got old.
His teeth fell out. He likes
to count them. I hear him
lining them up, sliding
each one across the wood.

Sometimes you feel like a monster
Or you dream you are
Or you dream you're an animal
And because you're not
You're so utterly human
That transformation takes on
Qualities of monsterhood
I guess
I mean I guess I shouldn't
Say you're a monster
I'm a monster
I feel like a monster with all
The mean thoughts I had today
I hung my head and had them
It wasn't like lying down
In the yard as a fox
It wasn't a dream
My propensity for cruelty
Which has yet to change my form

When monsters retire, I bet they move to the Amazon.

So few people and even if someone saw, if a woman saw,
in the colors of the jungle, in all the movement,

she would disregard it, say, *How funny! The wind and rain
turned a leaf*

*into a mouth of white teeth! Turned a bird
into an eye!*

*I stared too long for a second there
and poof! A figure.*

Could someone be there?

Is solitude carving someone out of the shadows for me?

No. Out of the sparkling spaces.

23

There's more than one monster.

I guess that's obvious.
But typically we consider one monster at a time.

Confrontation. The street. The bedroom.
You think, scream and run. Yell fire.

You think, punch the throat.
Knee the groin. Stomp the foot.

But I'm telling you,
there's more than one monster here

with you now. Against you.
You've considered this, too, haven't you?

You know there's nothing you can do.

You are hiding under the bed
in a monster's bedroom.
How the tables have turned!
What will you do first?
Make strange noises?
Grab at the monster's feet?
Sneak out and when
you're right behind the monster,
scream? Like the victim
you were once. Wait
until the monster's asleep and
fill the bed with scorpions.
Wait and then climb into bed.
Let him think he brought you here
without fuss. What a night.
What a position to be in.

One monster touches a cloud and asks,
Why not let the women shoplift formula?
Why not let the babies fill their bellies?

He touches the next cloud by accident.
He's flying with wings you'd describe as

grotesque. And look at the long fingers
he has between the stretches of skin.

That he thinks of small, hungry children,
is that irony? Is it a kind of taunting?

How can I think about monsters
when I woke up one day and
the forsythia were in bloom,
and then the maple tree had leaves,
and then the azaleas budded?
Sure, the butterfly's gone
that had been living on the patio,
and there was the afternoon
where I watched the two hawks
return to the tree over and over
for squirrels and nests of smaller birds.
Wasn't that the spring shaking its head
in despondency and contrition?
I sit and my lap fills with petals.

WATCHING TV, SEEING THE SHOT WOMAN

When I see the shot woman, a mother, with her child nearby, or in her arms,
I want to hold my son. I want to pick him up from school and hold him until
my heart stops hurting such that my brain tells me it's being flattened, folded,

when I know better. It's beating along as usual. Same fist-like shape as ever.
But not the sound I think, used to think of, *lub dub*, thudding, steady,
     muffled.

Since the cardiogram I know the sound is wet, bubbling, popping, and
every time I think of it, I feel sick. I'm uncertain about my body again for

the first time since my mother dissected a frog in front of me and I saw how
beautifully colored the organs can be. But then I was filled with excitement
at the body's potential and not nauseated by the secrets the body keeps.

If I go to pick up my son, I'll forget how badly I want to hold him in the car.
Through our evening of errands, dinner, bath time, I might not get to hold him

until bed. I will be tired. I will think of my own bed. Even as I hold him, I will
think of how to place his head back on the pillow, how to bring my arm back

along my own body. My elbow slips into the curve under my ribs. My whole
body is the infinite, the dips, the pivots—placeholders for the rest of my body.
An act of containment.

A POEM FOR MY SON

You're dead.

No. Sorry. This is difficult.
When the poem begins

I'm dead.

I'm dead and you're still alive
and I come back.

I come back

to see you. I come back
to tell you something?

I came back

to do something but
now that I'm here

I'm mourning

my lost body because
it is with my body that

I'd touch you.

Pitiful ghost.
Ghost who came here

to tell you

to forget the body, the skin.
Please.

But here you are. No. Here

I am, crying in the corner,
not your ghost,

—a ghost *for* you

to practice putting your
fingers through.

EASIER TO WRITE THE POEM
WHERE I'M THE QUEEN

I am in the royal bed.
I am not upset about anything
because my empire is upset
and I am busy with that.

My empire is at odds with the world
because it is perfectly at home in it.
It can't make a noise loud enough
to express its discontent.
Its frustration at the oversight
of surrounding empires
stands merely as all houses stand.
It is the embodiment of nothing
and the closest it has to a body
is me. Its unrest can be best described
as my displeasure.

I sleep in my crown.

I have heard the stories of my nearest
neighboring empire.
They made an armory in the basement.
They let the children touch the guns.

If I could speak better for my empire,
I would. I throw money at it.
I make sure everyone in it is happy.

Sometimes my empire sounds like
a whole family crying. Sometimes
it sounds like my son. This torn
state cannot stand. I feel like I'm being
reborn out of the tear in my empire
which looks like a vulva
because all tears look like vulvas.
Sometimes I spend weeks thinking
there are only phallic symbols.
But then the tearing.
And my new head is pressing forth
until it can be seen.

This new head wears the same crown.
And the crown is always worn
by the same head
in this empire and others.

When I pass through other empires,
I am the good queen: mouth and legs shut.
I can't bear a new child that would show
how we are all of blood.
The act of not bearing that child,
making it only a third of the way,
to, mostly, the blood—
no one would watch that.
And I can't arrange for my son to wed
their daughter such that my empire
will be at peace feeling
represented and cared for.

I enjoy the tea and presents.
I return home and cry as my empire is bereft
of the ear of any other empire.
As my empire is bereft a tongue.

IN FEBRUARY 2015

in a cemetery
the Jewish gravestones   pushed
toppled   overturned   uprooted
defaced
as many as 250

I think   if one of those graves
were mine   my ghost   would try
to recall   crying
the hunched spine   the body
heaving

I think   of the teens' determination
each time a grave   destroyed
a moment to reaffirm
yes another tiring
under the physical work of it

my ghost would   stretch   itself
so thin   crying
thinking it remembered
crying   stretched   and belly down
against the grass and stones

as many stones as it could touch
like a shroud   a way to grieve
as good as any
spread out   until the sea
and then   over it

spread out   until the first
living person   then over
the mouth
of that living   person
right over the mouth

MY OBSESSION WITH JUST IS
MY OBSESSION WITH THE TEMPORAL

Just ok / Just like that / Just like it / Just worry / Just there / Just so / Just as / Just because / Just observed / Just disparate / Just a part / Just trying / Just the paper / Just more / Just get / Just because / Just like / Just the flowers then / Or just / Just get / Just haven't / Just come back / Just in case / It was just that / It's just / Just once / I just want / Just after / Just an obituary / And just / Just more / You're just / Just not

THE WORLD

today the world is flat and the universe is small enough to contain a little square of a planet and yes it's deep enough to dig the graves and yes it's high enough to fly a plane but what else can you really tell at any one moment of your life nothing nothing more than that you little human in this little cube of a world so bring out a gun and shoot it up let's let it pour all over and force out the walls we can feel at every moment of the day even when we can see a horizon and we'll reshape it with that will we we'll turn it as big as we know it is as much as it frightens us as much as it ruins us and we'll need to be buried together at some point and scattered together at another and it's the cube making me morose it's the gun making me dead

DEAR GUN

Mostly I forget I've shot a gun,
but I took riflery at summer camp.
The first shot I took was so close
to the center of the target that
the counselor asked if I was sure
I hadn't shot a gun before. Yes,
I was sure. I blushed. I never
shot well again, and not because
I didn't want to. I liked lying there
with the rifle. I liked the target.
I liked competing with the boys
while most girls were in dance.
Dance class I could take at home.
Not riflery. Not the measured
distance in the woods. Not the
little turf laid out for us, our
stomachs. I worried more
about bathing in the lake than
the bullets or even how my arm
might ache, shoulder bruise.
But I don't think it did. I think my
body resisted it least. I don't think
I ever even imagined the target
as any wild thing—just the paper
it was. I don't want to shoot a gun
now, at a range. But I'd lie down
again with a rifle in the woods.
I'd imagine a little threat this time.
One I was always meant to hit.

HOW WE MIGHT SURVIVE

I'm the leg of my son across my back.
Which is to say, I'm the part of my back
under the leg of my son, as much as I can be.
I'm focused. I'm happy. I'm not

large enough to be the whole woman
in the whole world that seems complete only
when one end meets the other
in trauma. Not her. I'm only the small part

active in this sensation. Very still.
You might call it escapism but this is
how life works, trying to pull
us free, creating the break that we might

split ourselves upon. If we need to. Gently,
Here. Here. You are separate from the world.

NEUTRON STAR

At the museum, I stand on a scale that tells me how much I'd weigh on a
neutron star. (Trillions of pounds.)
I could walk the 20 miles around it in a day or two, except
not at that weight. Wherever I ended up on the star, that'd be it for me.

And also I'd be burned up faster than you can tut your tongue.
And also I'd be imploding from the pressure.

I guess I'd be a mess of ash pulled quickly to the surface.
And then that'd keep burning.

Neutron stars are the densest, but that's only because the ones with more
mass turned into black holes.
I'd rather not say those don't exist, that those anti-exist. I'd rather say
those are still dense stars, just more dense, more dense.

If we figure out teleportation, I can imagine the tests.
We set up a camera feed off a satellite, and we send a mannequin in a new
suit up there,
and we watch our equipment fail, and the mannequin disappears in a sort
of explosion, and we try again.

And once the mannequin holds up, we send a doll full of fluid. Then an
animal.
Then a bigger animal. And lots of them die despite our precautions. But
we figure it out.
And someone stands on the neutron star eventually.

Someone feels like trillions of pounds in a suit that's counteracting feeling
    like trillions of pounds
and rotating rapidly through the universe. And while they're gone one of
    the animals
that's returned safely dies from a complication no one and everyone
    foresaw.

And it's ok because the person standing on the neutron star expected that.
And it's ok because they don't believe in living on Earth anymore.

They don't believe in it at all.

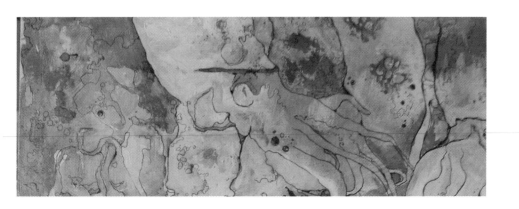

THE STARSHIP

What if you saw a starship?
If you went to a window and there she was.
The countless lights on her.
The endless night behind her.
The world dwarfed. You as well.

Well you do see her.
You imagine the people on the ship
as people because that's easiest.
You imagine the people on the ship floating
because you want to.

You would say she is above something
except she is above everything.
You know there must be an outline
to her shadow and that comforts you.
If you could just get far enough away,
you could trace her as a child would.
If you could just get far enough away,
then you wouldn't be here anymore.

A few days later your husband runs away.
He tries to take you with him
but you can see it's not much of a plan.
You can see how small he is,
the edge of the starship
in the window behind him as he tells you
which way he will drive the car.
When he can't convince you he asks
if he can take all the food bars.
Yes, you tell him.

Q

A few days after that
people still aren't leaving their homes
so the knock at the door startles you.
It's your neighbor.
When you look at him out the peephole,
he is looking at the starship.
You begin sleeping together.
It's easy to say fear
had something to do with it.
End times. Fleeting-ness.

After a few weeks go by
people go back to their jobs.
(There never would have been
an interruption in the local news
except no one wanted to go in.)
You go to the market and CVS.
People are still filling their carts
with water, but all you can think
about is how your husband
will undoubtedly return.

The plants in your yard are struggling
because of the shadow.
You drive out to the edge of it
and lie down with your body half in,
half out. And every ten minutes or so
you move a bit.
And when night comes it's kind of a relief.
And then you drive home.
You tell your neighbor how now
is the time to run away. Not before.

Everything isn't back to normal.
Just because you can go to stores again
and people aren't crying in the street.
You still can't sell your house.
You can't put it on the market.
You wonder how your husband
has made it this long.
If he doesn't return soon, you
will have to go to the bank
and decide how much money to keep.

Tonight you decide to enjoy it.
You make a margarita, go out back,
sit in a lounge chair, and watch the lights,
which are constant. This is how
you know they are not human.
At some point you need the dark.

When you used to talk to yourself,
now you talk to the ship. You sing her
little songs. *Gonna cook some chicken.*
Gonna remember the oil is heating
on the stove. A little less room for error,
living alone. No one but the ship to ask
if you can be hurt by the smell of burning.
Her response, *I can smell your house from here.*

The starship talks back more than you'd like.
I heard humans were more brittle, after you trip
and curse. You ask your neighbor if he imagines
her talking. He says he draws pictures of the aliens.
You say they might be humans from the future.
He says, *What would I do with all these tentacles?*

You see a headline about where
new cars go to die, to control supply
with regard to demand, and you like the word
demand, and you like the phrase *where blank
goes to die*, and you wonder if the starship
came here to die. Like a Jeopardy answer—
What is Earth? What is Earth?

Q

Your neighbor's wife left your neighbor
long before the starship. She wanted children.
When he proposed to a woman who wanted children,
he thought that feeling would come with age.
He was embarrassed he was wrong.
You used to talk to his wife when you caught
each other in the yard, coming home from work.
More privately, you used to hear her yell about lost years.

Your neighbor's wife probably has a child now.
You wonder how she feels about that with
alien invasion in every news broadcast. They keep
showing pictures of the ship taken with the best
telescopes and there's never movement. You dig
your childhood telescope out of the basement
and try to get a better look for yourself. But when
you've been watching for an hour, you know
you just like watching. Like having a beer in a museum.
Because you have nothing to lose.

More recently the news is about world leaders
meeting to discuss if we should go to the starship.
What could get to her. What we might say
and how. You picture a fighter jet
painted with flowers and smiling stick figures.
You know smiling is a sign of aggression to
chimpanzees or gorillas, right? Maybe
just the flowers then. Or maybe
we should leave well enough alone.
Keep signaling with Beatles songs on radiowaves
and light shows and our continuing lives.

You wonder if they've already sent jets up to her.
Why would they broadcast something so
unpredictable? They must have at least
tested small rockets to see if they would
burn up, reaching a forcefield. Maybe the FBI is
destroying footage right now. Maybe
they're shooting different wavelengths at her
to catch a glimpse of her shields. See if they can
make them shimmer like a splashed puddle.
They're thinking so narrowly again.

Q

You buy a sun lamp. You set it on the table
between you and your neighbor
and you laugh. *You're so bright!* You are!
Should we grow marijuana in my living room?
No, that's with heat lamps. *Oh.*
But I have some weed if you want. *Yes!*
And he leaves and you realize
your eyes are already used to it.

You lie on a big blanket in the backyard
and smoke and eat cookies and stare at her.
Your neighbor says he can feel the light
from her. Your neighbor brings up
the twinkling of stars. In a moment of clarity,
you figure out why the ship has come,
why the ship is empty. It's for you. It's for
everyone. It's an evacuation of your planet,
but she won't take you unwillingly.

You roll over to tell your neighbor,
and he's asleep. You tell him anyway,
or you tell the starship, or just, you say it aloud—
I'll go. I'll do it. I don't think I'd mind.
You hear a car pull up to the house,
and you know your husband is home.

You don't know how long it takes him to find you
in the back, but now he's here. He lies down
next to you, but not between you
and your sleeping neighbor. He says, *I'm not mad.*
He says, *I can tell.* As if he knew you were thinking,
This could be platonic. And you roll over and wrap
your arms around him. You've missed him
so you say, *I've missed you.*

When you wake your neighbor is gone but
your husband is still there. Last night
that seemed right. Now you don't know.
The only thing you're sure about is the starship.
You're the only thing I'm sure about,
she says. You smile at her.

Your neighbor sees you're awake
and waves you over. *What are you going to do?*
he asks. *Nothing.* But he says, *Not about me.*
About the ship. And you like him more
for that. He's still got things in perspective.
He says, *I want to go, too.*
Which you should've expected him to say.

This is how the discussion goes with your husband:
What about our kids? Or, we were going to have kids.
What about our jobs? We could still become something.
Not like before. Ok. But what if you go up there
and they're not saving us. What if they're going to
experiment on you? Or eat you? Or what if that ship
breaks? Or they didn't stock enough food and you
have to make choices about who to eat? Would you eat
someone? I'm sorry. I sound like a bad movie.

You tell your husband all the decisions seem
the same. Maybe not if you already had a child,
but you don't. And could you have a child now,
here, with the history of the ship in the history
of Earth? No. Leaving is your best shot at
feeling settled again, your best shot at children
and laughing while you roll around together
in the grass—well, not grass—on a big bed, say.
And you want that. You've thought about that
for a very, very long time.

○

Your husband says, *I want to go with you*
if that's where you see a stable life.
Something that resembles the future
we've always talked about. And I understand
that having children here feels like
dooming them to a dying planet
even if we'd live our lives to the end
hardly seeing change.

But he keeps going. Hold your breath.
But I'm scared. And I would be scared
for a long time. And I don't know what
kind of person I am when I'm scared.
I can only imagine that I'm awful and,
by the time we arrived anywhere,
I'd have destroyed us. And so we still
wouldn't end up with the life I've been
holding onto. And if either way I end up
without you, then it's easier to stay.

Before long there's a TV crew in the starship.
She's empty. There's air, water, food, clothes,
rooms with beds. Even playground
equipment in what looks like common areas.
Turns out you just get an aircraft close enough
and she pulls it into a landing bay.
They can't broadcast from in there,
but when they air it later it feels like
it was live. You and your husband are
mesmerized. For a second, he's tempted
by the beauty of the design. But you
wish he wouldn't admit that out loud.

Soon enough people are going on TV to announce
their decisions to travel on the ship,
or at least to live there, to wait. Scientists mostly.
The governments are setting up online systems
to sign up, keep track. You have to say your
profession. You have to pay $200. At first some
countries are nervous they will lose
all their scientists, but people are different enough.

Q

The plane you take up is like every other plane ride.
A baby is crying. Some people that know each other
are chatting. Some strangers are introducing
themselves. Many people are drinking, or were
at the airport bar. You were encouraged to pack light.
You have a photo of you and your husband
at the Grand Canyon. You have a necklace
from your mother. You have a lot of Twizzlers
and dark chocolates. Your husband said if people
found out they might kill you for them
further into the trip, when they miss Earth.

Your neighbor took an earlier flight
and he's there to greet you.
He's so excited to tell you about
everything. He takes you to the room
he's saved for you, beside his, and
makes a joke about being neighbors
everywhere. His enthusiasm is the first
thing that's made you doubt yourself.

First you notice how small the beds are.
You've been sharing a bed with a man
for years. This will be the biggest change
for you, but you get it. It's as if the aliens
are saying, We're happy to have you
but this isn't a good time to get pregnant.
And you wonder about the medicine
on board. You wonder if doctors volunteered
to come on the ship. You wonder
if you're of any use at all.

The ship stays still for months. Some
people change their minds and return
home. Some people come up to her
for vacations. Your husband visits.
He brings more chocolates. You have
protected sex on the small bed.
He likes your room, notes the picture
you've hung, notes the lack of color,
can't seem to stop running his mouth.

You tap the trim and it turns purple,
tap it again, yellow. Various parts
of the room respond. You just haven't
decided what to do yet. He's being
snide when he says decisions
aren't usually a problem for you.

Just come back, he says. *What*
do you even do all day? Aren't you
getting depressed? But you aren't.
There's a lot to explore. And you've
been reading. And mothers need help
with their children. The people
on board are thinking of setting up
jobs with mentors to teach them—
nurses, police officers, teachers.
You think you'll be a police officer.
You think you'd like to do some good.

What does that even mean? Are there
laws? Are there guns? Are there trials?
You say you'd patrol. You'd help
whoever needs help. More like
a neighborhood watch than police. But
there are a set of rooms they've found
that can't be opened from the inside
just in case.

You find a dead moth in your room.
It must have stuck on a bag or even
your clothes. Or your husband's.
You wonder if you've done things all wrong.
If this was supposed to be an ark.
Animals and plants and insects and
the right people to mind them.
Haven't you had time to coordinate that?

You're glad though. You'd be worried
if there were lions on board. Rhinos.
Even cats. They stopped those
at the airport. You would be allergic
so you're glad for that too. You might
have allergies wherever you're headed.
You might die an awkward, pointless,
human death among aliens who
did their best preparing for your arrival.

You decide to keep the dead moth.
It amassed enormous sentimental
value in the second it took
to figure out what you were seeing.
You haven't missed insects up here,
but you like moths. You like how they
start as caterpillars. And you like
the metamorphosis. And you like most
the hours hanging on the cocoon
while the wings dry out.

Suddenly the ship turns blue. The lights,
the walls, the trim you'd set at navy—
all a light blue. You think you're the only
one to guess this means *prepare*
for departure but of course everyone
is talking about it. For you, it's a little
different. For you, you hear the ship tell
you—in the sweet voice you've given her
that's gotten sweeter since you got here—
Go to your room, little animal.

Now you know which time was the last time
you saw your husband. You can't help
crying even though you hardly like him anymore.
How funny how different a person he was
in the different lives available to him.
How you might never have known that.
How the ship revealed him in a way you never
needed to know. How you might think the ship
cruel if you didn't feel, with some certainty,
like you were being saved.

Q

The ship is blue for about four days.
100 hours. And then it leaves. And then
certain windows show the blackness
of space and countless stars. And no view
shows an edge of Earth. You hold
your hand up to a window and you don't
know how to talk about the speed of the ship
or how it distances you from your husband.
But you know if you ever return,
he will likely be dead.

Your neighbor says he doesn't understand
your relationship anymore without the nights
drinking in the backyard. So you lead
him to a common area, with a high ceiling,
that many rooms overlook in a sort of cylinder
above. You lie down, and he lies down too.
Finally, the lights are changing, you say,
as people move in and out of the rooms above.
You imagine the ship flickering through space.

It's not long before you've stopped again.
At the windows you see the ground of a new planet.
You see water. You see that plants are moving
in what you would call wind. You see aliens,
but they're so small from this height.
You expect a rush to the ship. Warm greetings.
Introductions. Names given to every new thing
you can see. But their response is the same
as Earth's was at first. They wait.

They're more advanced than humans. After
they waited, they must have decided to board,
and then they're here. Easy. You go to where
the ship pulls in the smaller ships. You watch
from a window. They come armed, and they
threaten you in their language. But they realize
you know nothing. No one does. To them,
it's as if they, too, were sent an empty ship.

They leave a few armed guards to watch,
but most of them return to their planet.
You go up to one of the guards and try
to talk to him, but it's more difficult
than you'd imagined. So you hold up
your right hand. You grab a finger and say,
Finger. Then you count, *One, two, three,
four, five. I have five fingers. One, two, three,
four, five*. He understands. He counts
your fingers. You learn five new words.

Then the fanfare begins. Aliens come, recording
and curious. Alien children visit. You do your
best to say hi and introduce yourself to anyone
who stops. You let them touch your hair and
your skin. They look closely at your eyes. When
you get nervous you blurt out that they're round.
And then you get stuck trying to explain that
your eyes are perfectly round but hidden mostly
in your human head. You're so glad when they
give up trying to understand your gestures
which probably look like you're punching yourself
in the face.

They always all leave except for the guards.
It's disheartening. And then the ship turns blue.
You run to the guard and try to tell him.
The ship will leave in four days! But the days
are longer here. *The ship will leave soon!*
He doesn't know what you're saying, so you
countdown in his language, *Three, two, one,
boom!* And you throw your hand like a rocket.

The aliens come in three giant ships.
It's not that they weren't coming. It was just
that they were better managed,
better equipped. But, you guess, still,
they have nothing like the starship.
You feel like you could count them;
they're coming on so neatly.
But after you count the first hundred,
you feel sick and go to your room.

Is their planet dying too? This planet
you've watched for months. Did they
poison it? Or is it something inevitable
with the star that is their sun? Is it
a death that's still hundreds of years
away? Do they feel that passage of time
like you do? You have no trouble
imagining it and the ones you could've
loved, descended from you, living
how they shouldn't. Dying like that too.

All the constructs you've been working on.
The police watch, the nurses, etc. They all fail
when the ship is full of two different aliens.
Now when you walk quietly around the ship,
it's just for yourself. Though one time, just
once, you find a group of aliens restraining
one alien. And you show them the rooms
that lock from the outside. And they're
grateful to you. Though you're not sure who
should've been locked up. You wonder
if they have gender like humans do.

At the next planets, the story is similar.
You realize there's a long list of planets.
The ship will return when it's full.
How many different aliens by then?
You start to wonder if your husband
was right. This collection—a little science
experiment. You go back and forth between
worrying about that and all the dying planets.

Six planets. Six planets you watch for months
and then leave. Including humans, seven aliens.
The ship is noisy. Everyone has trouble
staying on a schedule together. Everyone sleeps
a little differently, a little longer or shorter,
or with breaks in the middle of the night. You
try to adjust to whatever planet you're on,
but the days spent traveling through space
are difficult. You're up late. You sit with people
who aren't people and try to learn a few words,
enough to tell a joke and hear a new laugh.

When you arrive at the last planet, your
destination, there's a ship there immediately,
filled with aliens who will help everyone
exit. They use a sound system that no one
even knew the ship had. *People of Earth. You
were the first on. You will be the first off. Gather
where the ships come in.* Then it's like
the Olympics, the message repeated in all
the other languages, calmly, like there's no rush.

You hadn't packed so you do it now.
You tear the photo off the wall. A drawing
your neighbor made of you sitting and talking
with the first aliens. You're nearly fluent
in their language now. You were less dedicated
about the others. Soon your bag is full
and on your back and you're waiting.

To get to the ground, you take a space elevator.
You'd read about these on Earth. That's
something you'll be doing a lot now: adding
on Earth to the ends of your sentences.
You would've been so impressed with
the space elevator ride two years ago, three,
however long it's been. But now—in the shadow
of your arrival—they're forgettable minutes.

You can't believe how different
the planet feels from the ship.
The dips and mounds, the give
beneath your feet. And air
that moves. Your hair moving.
And sunlight. You love that
the word is the same. You love
how it feels on your skin even if
it's colder out than you've felt
in years. You get goosebumps.

You're directed to a tent with *Earth*
written on it. Inside it's filled
with paraphernalia. It's heartwarming,
and callous too. You go up to someone
behind a table with a calendar on it.
Do you look human for our benefit?
Do you think we'd freak out
if we saw you? He laughs. *No,*
he says. *We're humans.*

You learn they're humans from the future.
The starship breaks time and space
and they sort of choose where to come
back into it. They are time travelers.
Which means they could take you back.
You don't think of that immediately
but you think of it.

Walking around you notice people here
speak a dialect of English. They've learned
the old dialect to help you. They have so
many people speaking so many languages,
you have to leave the tent. It's too much.
You go and lie under a big plant. It's green
because as long as there's a sun
photosynthesis makes sense. It's a smart,
simple evolution. And that calms you.

Your neighbor finds you under the plant, but
he might not be your neighbor anymore.
You hold hands. He's been asking questions
too, and he's found out this is the second
planet they inhabited after Earth. They picked
it for size and atmosphere and water and
the energy and lifespan of this universe.

They explain that we can live longer
if we want. Their medical advances
are significant. They explain that crime
is not tolerated, and that racism, sexism,
and other prejudices are criminal. They
will provide therapy to anyone who
recognizes they need help to adjust.
And it is hard to believe. All of it.

They have built apartments, similar
to the ship, while you figure out how
you fit in here. What job. What classes.
What openings. Where. And then
a new place to live. A yard again.
The apartments would be too similar
to the ship if not for the windows.
Even so, your first time looking out,
you think, *Mirage.*

Your neighbor asks if you will
try to buy a house together
after you find jobs. *We can
pick it based on the yard.*
Here's the conversation you
didn't want to have. But part
of you didn't believe you would
make it this far. And weren't
the last years sort of lovely?

You say it as plainly as you can.
I want kids. Now that we made it.
I want kids. Here. You think
that'll be the end of it. But he says,
Me too. And you can't stop yourself.
I don't believe you. Or I believe you
but nine months is a long time,
and I don't believe your desire is . . .
steadfast. He says, *Steadfast?*
What am I? A sea captain?

⦿

He makes it easy to turn to jokes.
I just want to date some future humans.
He says, *Who can blame you?*
And that's the last you talk about it.
You thought the romantic part of you
would've been killed as punishment
for abandoning your husband,
but you find yourself thinking, if we're
meant to be, it could still happen.

You start dating a man who
names all the flowers for you.
It seems easier to fall in love
on this planet. There's not one
man who doesn't respect you
or doesn't think you deserve
equal pay or reproductive rights.
You get a job at a museum
and you move into his house.

You ask why he was still single and he confesses
that he was waiting for the starship's return.
His childhood was full of nothing but talk of the ship.
Preparations and dying planets and it led him
to stories of Earth. He read so many old novels.
You realize you're sleeping with a fanatic, an Earth fanatic.
Like you're a rockstar. You're not sure if he would
love you otherwise. But that's lucky for you.

He doesn't like that you were married before.
Divorce is so rare now. And you're not divorced.
You're technically married to a man in the past,
on the planet your new lover obsesses over.

But that's not true. He probably
filed for divorce and checked off
some box: ❏ Left on a starship.
And it was granted to him by a judge,
nodding in his black robes.
Then you realize, in some way,
most ways, entirely, based on
the understanding of time you're
familiar with, were raised with,
your husband is dead.
And you're a widow.

Your lover works in surveillance.
It's a big industry. The way he explains it
reminds you of the time you got
a ticket in the mail for a traffic violation
caught on camera in the middle
of the night. A long red near your house
that seemed silly to wait for. Your lover
delights in your story of Earth.

When your lover named the flowers,
he also talked about the history
of naming flowers. He said,
On the second planet the names
were awful. So many named after
the people who studied them.
Can you imagine plants named
Freeman and Stein? And then
a lot named New whatever. New
Dandelion. New Geranium.
New Rhododendron was beautiful.
The plant. I can show you pictures.

On this planet, we had a naming committee
to make sure the names were beautiful
and pleasant. And we decided,
if they wanted to reuse Earth names,
they could, without distinction.
Most of the names are practical, too. Like
the trees that smell like Jasmine,
they're Jasmine Shade. And Remarawound.
That one's poisonous.

The whole time the starship is still in the sky,
but higher. No giant, plant-killing shadow.
You still talk to her. You mention to your lover
that she must be lonely, so empty.
And he says that there are tons of people up there,
working, preparing her for the next trip.
He says, *We're still going through*
the surveillance. You stop breathing.
You think someone would die up there
and we wouldn't know who to hold accountable?

Don't worry, he says. *What you would call*
a computer reviews most of it. We know
what's private. But you don't know if
a computer can be programmed
to distinguish between consenting and
non-consenting. You don't know
what sex looks like for the aliens
who were on board. You never thought
to ask your lover if you have sex
differently from future-women. If you
orgasm in some old-fashioned way.

Did anyone die up there?
Yes, he says, *but no one*
was murdered. You ask,
Why didn't anyone come
and greet us and explain?
He says, *We wanted to*
have as little impact as
we could. The ship was
nearly forgotten this way.
No history affected.

Can I read somewhere the history
of the years just after the ship left?
He says, *Of course*, and brings it up
on a tablet. Notable events of later
that year: another mass shooting,
a factory exploding, fires in Colorado,
a new all-electric car from Honda,
and the first woman President.
You cry reading about everything.

Q

You don't have to ask if you can
look someone up. You figure it out.
One night you stay up late and
read what you can find about
your husband. Just an obituary.
He remarried, was survived by two
of three children, spent his retired
years in local government. He died
of cancer, but he seemed happy
in that paragraph-long description
of his life and death.

Did you have to kill aliens to take
over this planet? you ask. He laughs.
No. We picked a young planet.
There's a lot of life in the water, but
it hasn't evolved much yet. We're excited
to see how it will. Eventually. I mean, we
won't see it. I can't imagine. But someone
will, if we do well in populating
and sustaining this planet. And they'll
keep a record. And someday you'll be
able to watch the evolution of a new
being as a stop motion movie.

Q

You work at the Space Museum.
You've always loved museums
but they were too familiar on Earth.
You couldn't imagine working among
the same information, the same pieces,
day after day. But here you know next
to nothing. And the museum is huge.
Whole wings are like art museums,
dedicated to the art of different worlds.
It's the most magnificent place
you've ever seen. It alone could
convince you to leave Earth again.

One day you finally ask,
Why did you bring us here?
And he answers plainly,
There aren't enough of us.
He keeps eating dinner.
That's it? And after he
swallows, *Yes. We have*
this perfect society, finally,
but not enough people for it
to flourish. And there are
always dying planets.

Q

Why is it perfect? Where are
the power hungry? The people
who feel they aren't getting
what they deserve and then
are lashing out? How? How
is that possible? Your lover
starts trying to explain,
but you can't stop.
Why would you risk
all that coming back
by bringing us here?

I guess we're still arrogant.
And just the slightest humor
eases you and the tremendous
pressure in your chest
at the thought of a world
contaminated by everything
that terrified you, every
reason you wanted to raise
a child in a new world
if given the chance.

Q

So you marry this man
after a few years. Maybe
because he's the one,
maybe because you're
tired of feeling like
your life is halted,
as if this giant stone
beast is blocking the way,
holding up his hand.
You've been breaking
your nose on that hand
for years, so to speak.

Maybe that's why you haven't
felt beautiful in all that time.
But that doesn't stop you
from getting pregnant.
You're pregnant for so many
days because days are shorter
here, if only slightly. It's a long,
lonely time when you can't
feel lonely because you are
always together. And so,
somehow, it's also joyful.

Q

The doctors marvel at you,
all your old-human complaints,
like the swelling in your hands
that you can hardly see but that
has you wearing braces
at night. They bring up old
textbooks to read about
the pregnancy you'd imagined.
The hospital bed, the IV,
the monitors around the belly.
They don't have the old tech,
but they'll do what they can.

You have a baby girl.
She's healthy.
She breastfeeds well.
You don't. You bleed
and already
feel like giving up.
A nurse says, *Two weeks.*
At the two-week check-up,
you won't have any
complaints. It won't hurt.

Your neighbor has a daughter
about the same age. You
spend afternoons with his wife,
the two babies lying near
each other on the floor, both
of you shaking toys over
their sweet faces. Or they sleep
and you two talk. But when
she asks about your neighbor's
old wife, you say you don't
remember her anymore.

All the things you thought
you'd have to teach a daughter
about her period and condoms
and rape and watching her drink
at parties—you don't have to
here. You know it's relief
you're feeling but it feels like
you fell, quick enough to
reach the bottom of a well,
and all you can do is look up.

You take your daughter to the museum
where you work and introduce her
to your co-workers as you walk around
the halls with her. They coo over her.
She sleeps most of the time. You love
the sight of her body next to the alien art.

Your husband's heartbeat is a little
slower than yours. But you don't
listen to your own heartbeat.
It's more accurate to say that his
heartbeat is slower than that
of your first husband, whose heart
you also listened to, at night, in bed,
in the pauses in conversation.

You put your daughter down for a nap
and you put your ear to her chest.
You hear her heart race. And lying
like that, it feels like you're waiting
for it to slow down. But you're not.
For God's sake, you're not.

Sometimes you think you've forgotten
about God except for how he's in
your speech. Not that they don't pray here.
They do. They have the idea of God you
have from when you studied mysticism
in middle school. An idea that has
to do with energy. And they see prayer
as mindfulness and an expression
of gratitude. The moments they spend
silent in temples seem to buzz and
it feels like you're touching people
who you're not touching. A loss of self.

Q

Almost everyone chooses to live longer
than any life you expected to live,
but no one chooses to live forever, as
a kind of computer program, even though
the technology is available. They
want to go into the energy. *Exist another*
way, says the starship, trying to explain.
You don't know what you'll do.
You might let your daughter decide.
You might let her keep you.

For now, you lie with your daughter in the yard
and listen to the pollinators. So far from Earth
and still pollinators. Flying around, making
sure the plants meet other plants and continue
to grow. You tell her about bees, their yellow
and black stripes, their stingers. How, as a girl,
at school, if a bee came near, everyone froze.
Almost every child that could hear its buzzing
froze where they were and waited,
until someone ran.

Q

You know you've been looking for something
to be wrong. You've seen too many episodes
of *Dr. Who* and *Star Trek*. You can't help
imagining yourself at the center of a story.
You can't help words like *hero* and *destiny*
entering your head. But nothing is wrong.
Or only little things, spats with your husband,
trouble opening a jar, the loss of a privacy
you once had (but you don't even mind that).
You know at some point you'll relax,
and you're waiting for that point now.

Clipping your daughter's toenails
makes you want to clip your husband's.
See if they curve, bend over the toe, in
the same way as hers. Different from yours.
In a moment she seems foreign to you
and that feels dangerous. But
the moment passes so quickly that
you don't even remember feeling that way.

Q

Honestly, the danger has come and gone like that
countless times. It is beginning to have a cumulative
effect that you feel as restlessness. You don't know
where it comes from. *And how could you?*
says the starship. You've got your daughter asleep
in your arms in a chair in the backyard,
and as you look up at the starship you know
you could see her from almost anywhere.

Your husband surprises you with a daytrip
to an ocean, to a reef, even if that's not the word,
and you have spots reserved on a submarine
with giant observation windows. You wear
your daughter strapped to your chest, facing
out, and you hold her little feet as you board.

It's the first big ship you've been on since
the starship. You pause. You hesitate.
And when you realize what you're feeling
is fear, you realize that your journey on the starship
was a trauma. At least, that's how your body
is recalling it now.

In some ways these views of the life
under the ocean are more spectacular
than all those views of space.
Your neighbor would disagree but
he's not here. *There's just more color,*
you can hear yourself saying.
And when you want to name everything
for your daughter, but you don't know
the names, you end up describing,
excitedly, the scene of color. *Look
at that red, baby. Vermillion!*

On the ride home you read about
the names of all the species of all the fish
they've discovered so far. You wonder
if you can get plush toys of them
so your daughter will grow up with
the right words. You remember
you once tried to find an octopus toy
in all your old toys at your parents'
and you found seahorses, jellyfish,
dolphins, whales, turtles—but no octopus.
And now you're just a walking dictionary
of the archaic language of Earth.

You decide to run away with your daughter.
It shouldn't come as a surprise to you,
but it does. And you know you're not really
running away. He'll know where you are.
But even then, he won't come after you.
You're not in love like that. And it's just not
a human trait anymore—abandonment.
He'll keep expecting your return. And you'll
say things to promote that. You can see it now,
how you two will stay in touch, cordially.
And you still won't have to go back.

Q

You can raise your daughter by yourself.
She's walking now. She crawls out of her room,
pulls herself up on the doorframe, and walks
into the room at your applause and laughter.
You two can do anything together. And there's
a whole infrastructure to support any choice
you make. You hold her hand with the plan
in your head and you can feel this new world's
potential. In the steadiness of its systems, it needed
one unpredictable being. And your life bursts
triumphant through a stitch.

ACKNOWLEDGMENTS

Sincere thanks to the editors of the following journals, who published many of these poems, often in earlier versions, sometimes with different titles:

American Poetry Review: "A Poem for My Son," "How We Might Survive," and "The World"

Arsenic Lobster: "Two Oaks" and "In February 2015"

Bennington Review: "You Are Connected to Everything"

Berfrois: "The Starship"

Connotation Press: An Online Artifact: "Dear Gun," "I Thought It Was a Good Idea to Walk to CVS with My Son on a Ninety-Degree Day," and "Watching TV, Seeing the Shot Woman"

Day One: "Everything Small"

Horsethief: "Easier to Write the Poem Where I'm the Queen" and "Retribution"

Kenyon Review: "Neutron Star"

Poetry Northwest: "The E-Ray Is a Gun"

PoetsArtists: "My Obsession with Just Is My Obsession with the Temporal" and "Mothers"

The Rumpus: "For Max"

Slice: "Suicide Prevention"

Storyscape: "Mouths at the Party," "The Safety of Women," and "A Threat"

TriQuarterly: an excerpt from "The Starship"

West Branch: "One Doctor Leads to the Next" and "Rats"

"Rats" was reprinted at *Verse Daily* and *Poetry Daily*.

"A Threat" was a Web Weekly Feature at *Verse Daily*.

"Easier to Write the Poem Where I'm the Queen" was featured on the interdisciplinary mixtape *Idols + Enemies* by Lushlife.

Thank you to Noah and Aaron. To my family. To Catie Rosemurgy, Lynne Beckenstein, Linda Gallant, Rachel Mennies, Natalie Shapero, Eleanor Stanford, Max Ritvo, Kimberly Quiogue Andrews, Evan McGarvey, Shane McCrae, Sarah Yake, Todd Davis, William Woolfitt, Hila Ratzabi, Justin Boening, Roxanne Ward, and Laura Kochman. To a small workshop with Amorak Huey, Tanya Grae, Ashley Nissler, Charmi Keranen, Linda Dove, Jesse Clemens, Susan Pigman, Michael Cherry, Naoko Fujimoto, Mary Westcott, and led by Jill Alexander Essbaum. To those who supported "The Starship" especially—C. Russell Price, Carmen Giménez Smith, Jennifer L. Knox, Corey Zeller, Russell Bennetts, Shuwei Fang, Brian Spears, Sumita Chakraborty, Andrea Rochat, Goodloe Byron, Lynne DeSilva-Johnson, Peter Oravetz, Michael Pattison, Holly Burdorff, Michele Harman, Danielle Susi, Lynne Kovalchik, Caits Meissner, and Nicky Arscott.

Special thanks to Suzanna Tamminen, Stephanie Prieto, and the rest of the team at Wesleyan University Press. And thank you to the National Endowment for the Arts.

ABOUT THE AUTHOR

SARAH BLAKE is the author of the poetry collection *Mr. West*, founder of the online writing tool Submittrs, and a recipient of an NEA Literature Fellowship. Her poetry has appeared in *Kenyon Review, American Poetry Review*, and *The Rumpus*. She lives outside Philadelphia, Pennsylvania. An online reader's companion is available at www.wesleyan.edu /wespress/readerscompanions.